WORLD ECONOMY EXPLAINED

Money and Credit

Sean Connolly

amicus

Published by Amicus
P.O. Box 1329
Mankato, MN 56002

Printed in the United States of America, at Corporate Graphic'
in North Mankato, Minnesota.

Library of Congress Cataloging-in-Publication Data
Connolly, Sean, 1956-
  Money and credit / by Sean Connolly.
    p. cm. -- (World economy explained)
  Includes index.
  Summary: "Explains the functions of money and credit"--Provided by publisher.
  ISBN 978-1-60753-081-7 (library binding)
  1. Money--Juvenile literature. 2. Credit--Juvenile literature. I. Title.
  HG221.5.C656 2011
  332.4--dc22

                                                        2010001379

Created by Appleseed Editions Ltd.
Designed by Helen James
Edited by Mary-Jane Wilkins
Picture research by Su Alexander

Photograph acknowledgements
page 7 Tony Vilches/Alamy; 9 Basque Country-Mark Baynes/Alamy; 10 Alfredo Dagli
Orti/British Museum/The Art Archive; 12 Photos 12/Alamy; 14 A ROOM WITH
VIEWS/Alamy; 15 Schenectady Museum; Hall of Electrical History Foundation/
Corbis; 16 Carrie Villines/Alamy; 19 Jeff Greenberg/Alamy; 20 Mary Evans Picture
Library/Alamy; 21 Kamyar ADL/Alamy; 23 Matt Griggs/Alamy; 24 Trinity Mirror/
Mirrorpix/Alamy; 27 Barry Stow Architect; 29 Bettmann/Corbis; 31 Reuters/
Corbis; 32 World History Archive/Alamy; 34 YM Yik/epa/Corbis; 36 Catchlight
Visual Services/Alamy; 39 Nick David/PFEG; 40 Courtesy Barclays Bank; 43 Bjoern
Sigurdsoen/epa/Corbis
Front cover imagebroker/Alamy

DAD0039
32010

9 8 7 6 5 4 3 2 1

Contents

Understanding Money

People have been fascinated by money for as long as it has existed. Think of some of the sayings, songs, and advice you've heard about money. "Money makes the world go round." "Money, money, money—it's a rich man's world." "The love of money is the root of all evil." "Neither a borrower nor a lender be." "A fool and his money are soon parted."

People have very different ideas about the value of money, and sometimes those differing attitudes sit side by side inside someone's head. A proverb that reflects how money can give a person influence over others goes: "He who pays the piper calls the tune." We can probably agree with that. Then again most of us would agree with the saying: "Health is better than wealth." Maybe we're not millionaires sailing around on huge yachts, but we're not suffering from a heart attack or other stress-related illnesses, either.

Can't Live with It…

The complicated nature of money makes it a necessary evil: as some people might say, "You can't live with it, but you can't live without it." That very complexity means that it is important that we all try to understand money. Individuals, families, and even countries base some of their most important decisions on how they treat money. If there is one thing about money that everyone can agree on, it is that money cannot be ignored.

In the middle of 2007, the world witnessed a massive upheaval that had money at its core. The focus was on credit—how easy or hard it is to borrow money—and this triggered one of the biggest economic crises in 80 years. What quickly became known as the credit crunch was the result of people making poor money decisions during the years which led up to it. The effects of the crisis will influence people's ideas about money (and credit) for many years to come.

Decades can pass between crises as serious as the credit crunch. During those interim periods, money continues to occupy people's thoughts—influencing political decisions, affecting jobs, defining how much houses are worth. Young people know that money will loom large when they become adults.

This book examines the many aspects of money and seeks to explain how it works, as well as how people can lose sight of both its power and its limitations.

Prices are marked in euros in this Italian farmers' market. Italy used a currency called lira until 2002, when it changed to euros.

Fair Exchange

We use money to pay for goods—

objects such as food, houses, clothing, and computer equipment. We also use it to buy services, such as entertainment, education, and insurance. We have a huge choice of ways to pay, but every transaction involves money passing from one person (or company) to another. Whether we hand coins to a vendor, or type bank details on a web site, an agreed amount of money changes hands.

People who lived in the earliest cultures many thousands of years ago would have found the idea of exchanging coins and notes for something they wanted baffling. Neither paper money nor coins have any obvious value. They only become valuable and useful when national governments say they are valuable, and if people in those countries agree on that value. But how did societies develop this method of buying and selling goods?

Barter and Trading

People throughout history have always exchanged goods and services. Schoolchildren exchange trading cards, marbles, and even parts of their lunch. Without knowing it, they are using the same system of exchange as some of the earliest human societies—a system called barter.

In early societies people traded goods (often food) with each other using a barter system. A fisherman might trade a trout for a large melon. The deal would be made on the spot, perhaps after some bargaining. Even in modern societies, people sometimes swap items such as books or furniture—even houses—without using money. By doing so, they are continuing an age-old tradition. But straightforward bartering has not always been easy, or even possible.

Spanish schoolboys swap sports cards.
The urge to trade goods is basic and
universal, with traders hoping to
improve their position after a "deal."

Even in simple societies that used barter systems, complications could arise. What happened if a fisherman wanted two melons from a farmer, but the farmer did not need two trout? If the farmer took two trout home, one might spoil before he could eat it. People needed a way to store the value of the fish and the melons, so that both could buy what they wanted when they wanted it.

Assyrian merchants transport goods on horseback. Middle Eastern peoples such as the Assyrians were using money more than 4,000 years ago.

The solution for many cultures was to use valuable items, such as precious metals or shells, called commodities, to store agreed amounts of value. The commodities had to be relatively scarce, which is why salt and gold were used, rather than acorns or sand. Some societies may have used commodities as money as many as 100,000 years ago; archaeologists have found stone containers of precious dyes among valuable goods.

Developing a System

As primitive societies developed into more advanced civilizations, their system of paying also became more developed. The area around present-day Iraq is often called the cradle of civilization. The ancient Babylonians used barley as the basis for their commodity money, and they created complex systems to use it that went far beyond simple exchanges between individuals. For example, by about 3000 BC people could use agreed amounts of barley to pay taxes and fines.

The first coins grew out of a similar tradition. Civilizations in western Asia and Africa, including the ancient Egyptians, used valuable metals as forms of payment and exchange. In about 650 BC, the kingdom of Lydia (on the west coast of what is now Turkey) began forming metals into round pieces that were stamped with the image of the ruler. These were the first coins.

The Lydians traded a good deal with their neighbors, including the ancient Greeks, who soon adopted the system of using coins to buy and sell goods. This was the dawn of modern money, and the gold and silver coins of the eastern Mediterranean Sea became the examples for other countries to copy. Later governments, from the Romans onward, built top-secret coin-producing factories called mints. Ordinary people often learned of a new king or queen because of the likeness they saw on new coins.

CLOSER EXAMINATION **CLOSER EXAMINATION** CLOSER EX

Clipping

Coins originally kept their value because they were supposed to contain a specific quantity of gold, silver, or another valuable metal. The stamp on the coin guaranteed that. But people often clipped little bits off the edge of coins to collect some of the metals, and still tried to get the full value from the clipped coin.

Look after the Pennies...

The coins we handle every day are part of a tradition that began almost 3,000 years ago. A penny with an image of President Abraham Lincoln on it tells the holder about the modern United States, just as a coin carrying the image of Julius Caesar revealed details about ancient Rome. The image shows where the power resides within a nation—either executive power in the case of the U.S. president, or full control in the case of Caesar.

This Roman coin from the first century BC honors Julius Caesar. Caesar was the military leader who extended Rome's control to the North Sea with his conquests of ancient France and Britain.

If you were to flip the two coins described on the previous page, you would learn even more. The reverse of a Julius Caesar coin might show Romulus and Remus, the legendary founders of Rome, or Aeneas, a Trojan warrior who was said to have been the ancestor of the Romans. The reverse of a penny coin depicts the Lincoln Memorial in Washington, D.C., which honors the 16th U.S. president.

National Statements

These images have several purposes. On one level, they identify the places the coins come from. But on another level, the traditional symbols add value to the coins. They act as a stamp of approval that tells people that the government produced the coins and can guarantee their worth.

That guarantee—or in some cases, promise—is important in the modern system of money. It also sets the modern system apart from those used until a few centuries ago. Most countries used commodity money—that is, coins containing amounts of precious metals— until the eighteenth or nineteenth centuries. Then as economies and populations grew, it became difficult for people to carry huge numbers of coins. In addition, producing the extra coins was expensive.

The next step was to use paper money (banknotes) as a form of representative money. In the past a coin had contained the metal that gave it value, but this new type of money was effectively a promise by the government to exchange the note for an agreed amount of a precious metal (usually gold).

Even that system became difficult to maintain, because banks or government treasury offices could not exchange large amounts of gold on demand. Governments then moved on to the type of money that nearly every country uses today—fiat money. The word fiat comes from the Latin meaning "let it be done." Notes can no longer be redeemed for gold, but the fiat decree makes it clear that the government expects people to use the notes as legal payment for all transactions.

This system underpins all other methods of payment, including credit cards, checks, and online transactions. Confidence in any country's currency is ultimately linked to confidence in its government and other institutions. That brings us back to the images of national symbols on the coins and notes we use.

An amateur archaeologist uses a metal detector to search for ancient coins and treasure in the country. Some finds are worth millions.

Personal Account

HOLDING A PIECE OF HISTORY

Historians and economists can find documents and theories to explain how business was carried out in bygone ages, but some people prefer a more hands-on approach to studying the past. Coin collecting is a hobby that gives people the chance to hold a piece of history in their hands. Dave Wood, a coin collector from Sussex, explains the attraction.

"What might this coin in your hand have bought two thousand years ago: was it used to buy bread, weapons, tools, or for gambling? The answer is probably all of these things. Coins may not talk beyond their portraits and legends, but they certainly unlock the imagination and allow you to mingle amongst people from millennia gone by."

Telling a Story

One of the most famous coins in history was struck by Brutus, one of the Romans who assassinated Julius Caesar in 44 BC. Brutus and his fellow conspirators called themselves the Liberators because they believed that Julius Caesar had assumed too much power. On March 15 (known to the Romans as the Ides of March) this group attacked Caesar with knives they had hidden in their clothing.

Brutus had coins made soon afterwards to mark the event. On one side of the coin was his own image. On the other side were the images of a cap (a Roman symbol of liberty) flanked by two daggers. Below was the inscription 'EID MAR' (Ides of March), a reminder that Rome's liberty was preserved on that date. The coins were used to pay Roman soldiers, reminding them that they were fighting for Roman liberty.

These two notes were printed by the Confederate States of America. This group of 11 states tried to become independent of the United States in 1861, but were defeated after a four-year civil war.

Credit Where Credit Is Due

Parents often explain finance by using examples from their children's experience. They might compare the family's decision to buy a car with their daughter's decision to buy a CD with her pocket money. Both purchases were made from a seller for an agreed price, and the transactions took place with no argument on either side.

This piggybank is stuffed with dollars. This image reflects the traditional view that adults should pay for big-ticket items—such as houses, cars, and furniture—by saving, just as children save their money in piggybanks. However, in the years leading up to the credit crunch, people were offered more and more credit to encourage them to make these purchases with loans.

There is one big difference between those two transactions. The daughter knew exactly how much money she had, so she paid for her CD with cash from her purse. Her parents, however, were hardly likely to walk into a car showroom, decide on a model, and start handing over thousands of dollars in cash. One way or another, they were likely to use credit to make the purchase.

Buy Now, Pay Later

Credit is a form of delayed payment, a promise by the buyer to pay back a debt at a later date. Most people use credit to make large purchases, such as buying a house or a car, so they can spread the payments over a period of time. People also use credit when they do not carry a lot of cash. Even a very rich person would be unlikely to pay for a motel room with cash.

The idea of using a promise to pay to complete a transaction goes back many years, almost as far back as money itself. European merchants used bills of exchange from Roman times to the Middle Ages to pay for goods when they reached foreign ports, rather than carrying large amounts of gold. A similar system used by Persian traders depended on slips of paper called *sakks*, which could be exchanged for money in countries as far away as China. Our word check also comes from that Persian word.

Checks, like those early forms of payment, depend on the payer having enough money to cover the amount to be exchanged. Modern credit goes beyond that and involves a second transaction, which is "buying" the money to pay for the first purchase. This purchase is called a loan, and it must be paid back over an agreed period. Just as importantly, the person who needs the money (the borrower) must pay an extra amount, called interest. This is, in effect, the price of that second purchase (to get the payment money). Loans for houses are called mortgages.

Credit cards also use interest as a way of letting people "buy" a bit more money. People receive monthly credit card statements listing all their purchases in the previous month. If they pay off the total amount, they pay no interest (and have been given up to a month to find money that they might not have had when they made some of the purchases). Any debt they carry over to the next month must be paid back with interest. Some people find it hard to control their credit card spending, which can lead to serious problems (see pages 20–25).

Personal Account

THE CREDIT-GO-ROUND

Sally (not her real name) is a single professional woman in her late twenties, who has had no formal financial training. However, she listens to the advice of friends who work in banks and other financial services.

"The first big thing I learned was that there's no real loyalty any more in this area. When I was growing up, I was led to believe that people opened a bank account and kept that same account active all their life.

"Maybe a person would get a credit card through the bank, and possibly a card with one of their favorite stores, but that would be it. If they ran up a big bill on a card, they'd be stuck with the problem of paying it off…

or face mounting interest. They wouldn't dream of going somewhere else for better credit.

"Then my banking friends started saying things like 'How close is your relationship with your bank? Does it help you manage your debts, or does it simply use every chance to slap on extra charges?' That was a bit of an eye-opener, coming from people working in banks themselves. The same people urged me to take up advertised offers to transfer the balance of one credit card to another, to reduce the interest on what's due. I began doing that about two years ago and have even switched from one of the cards I switched to then.

"It gets a bit confusing, this credit-go-round, but sometimes I think it's the only way to stay ahead of the game. It's hard to resist the temptation to just spend, spend, spend because of some attractive deal. That money needs to be paid back sometime, interest or no interest."

Web Accounts

Like many other industries, banks have begun to use the Internet as a way of expanding their business. Customers can go online to find bank details that would otherwise involve making a visit to the branch, calling them, or writing a letter. Many banking transactions, such as transfers and withdrawals, can now be done online, at any time of the day or night.

Some new banks exist only on the Internet. ING Direct and Virtual Bank are Internet banks that have no branch offices at all. They claim to be able to offer customers better rates because their overheads are so low. Other banks have a larger number of staff and hundreds of branches to maintain. The online banks offer 24-hour convenience instead of bricks and mortar.

A sign announces "Financing (credit) available" outside a group of new houses for sale in Florida. The photo was taken during the boom years of easy borrowing, before the credit crunch.

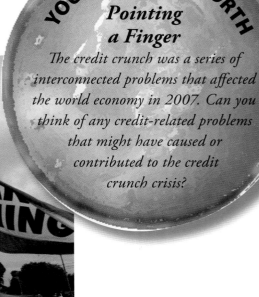

YOUR MONEY'S WORTH

Pointing a Finger

The credit crunch was a series of interconnected problems that affected the world economy in 2007. Can you think of any credit-related problems that might have caused or contributed to the credit crunch crisis?

Problems with Money

Money has the power to make people's lives easier (and some believe happier), but that power can also be harmful. This combination of potent forces has given money the power to influence people's behavior for better or worse. Most people believe their lives would be improved if they had more money. Many find it hard to deal with the problem of not having enough money.

A Measure of Worth

Most modern societies place a great deal of emphasis on the jobs people do to earn money. Some of this represents a genuine interest in what it is like to be, for example, a star athlete or a writer. But much of the curiosity and respect is linked to people's earning power,

Above: A homeless man sells the Big Issue *magazine outside a store in central London.*

or how much money they are paid in return for their work. When money becomes tight, people feel under pressure. The shortage of money might come about simply because someone is careless with his or her money.

Mr. Micawber, a character in Charles Dickens' novel *David Copperfield*, had this advice about money: "Annual income twenty pounds, annual expenditure nineteen pounds nineteen and six [about £19.97], result happiness. Annual income twenty pounds, annual expenditure twenty pounds ought and six [£20.03], result misery."

Opposite: Entire families could end up in debtors' prisons if they could not pay their bills in Victorian England.

Mr. Micawber was pointing out how fine a line there is between comfort and anxiety. In his view, the balance can be maintained through careful housekeeping, but people may run low on money because of circumstances beyond their control, such as losing a job, becoming sick, or because economic times are hard.

Bankruptcy

Sometimes people's debts mount up to the point where they cannot find a way to pay them back. This problem is as old as credit itself. Many countries use bankruptcy as a way of finding as fair a solution as possible between creditors (those who are owed money) and debtors (those who owe it).

People can choose to become bankrupt (this is known as filing for bankruptcy), or they can be forced into it by a creditor. Every country has its own rules on bankruptcy. A bankrupt person must then cooperate with a trustee, who examines the person's assets to see whether they can be sold to pay debts. Bankrupt people face many restrictions, so that they do not run up more debt. In some countries, they cannot use credit cards, become company directors, or even have bank accounts. A period of bankruptcy lasts for a specific period, and after that, the bankrupt person is discharged and allowed to resume activities that were banned during the bankruptcy. Although the trustee might have come up with a three to five-year plan for the debtor to continue paying some debts, others are wiped out.

The idea of bankruptcy arose in England during the reign of Henry VIII, nearly 500 years ago. It came about as a way of protecting creditors and ensuring that they could force a debtor to pay back money that was owed. The modern version still tries to help creditors to recover their debts, but it also offers some relief for someone who owes money.

Political battles are constantly being fought about how much a government—or society in general—should help people when they face financial hardship. Some argue that the government has a responsibility to support a wide-ranging welfare system that helps people retain their self-esteem, so that they can be ready to work when things improve. Others argue that too many government handouts go to undeserving people, who would prefer to live on benefits, rather than go out and look for work.

Too Much Money?

Perhaps it is hard to imagine having too much money, but many very well-off people (sometimes called the super-rich) have problems of their own, which less wealthy people might not even consider. One obvious problem is the constant threat of losing their money, for example, by being robbed. Thieves could be sizing up their expensive cars and boats, waiting to break into their luxurious houses, or plotting ways to cheat them out of their bank deposits. These fears may be coupled with anxiety about the risk of family members being kidnapped and their lives threatened unless a ransom is paid.

Enormous wealth may provide these people with possessions and financial security, but it also robs them of some freedom and adds extra layers of worry.

A security officer guards the gate leading to an upscale beach on the Caribbean resort island of Barbados.

A Healthy Balance

Mr. Micawber's thoughts about careful housekeeping on page 21 also apply to national economic policies. Most voters choose the political party they think will handle the nation's finances (or national income) best. They believe that all aspects of a nation's health and prosperity are affected by how carefully its government manages the country's finances.

Exactly where national income comes from is a matter of political debate within every country. Should the

British policemen battle with strikers during the coal miners' strike that threatened Britain's economy in 1972.

government raise taxes or cut costs? Even people who favor low taxes and few financial regulations agree that a national government has many financial responsibilities.

Forming Policies

A national government can be compared with someone who runs a household and looks after the family budget. Schools and hospitals need to be built or repaired, just as families need to buy clothing and food. Education is a big concern for both—the government makes decisions about training and paying teachers, while a family may need to buy computers and other equipment to help pupils through their school years.

All these decisions are affected by the budget— the precise amount of money coming in and going out. Families add money to their budgets through their income (money they earn) and their investments. Governments use the money raised by various taxes to pay for expenditures that they believe are necessary or unavoidable.

Just as individuals and families choose to borrow money for their largest purchases (for example, car loans and mortgages), governments also borrow money. Most governments do this by issuing government bonds, which are like loans. The bonds are usually for a set amount of the national currency. U.S., Canadian, or Australian bonds are in dollars, and British bonds are in pounds sterling.

The people who buy the bonds are actually lending the country the money they pay for the bonds. They expect a certain amount of interest to be paid on their investment, either at regular intervals, or after a specific

YOUR MONEY'S WORTH

Costs and Benefits?

Governments raise much of the money that they need to spend through taxes that people pay on the money they earn (their incomes). Taxes are also paid by businesses, by customers buying alcohol or tobacco, or by car owners paying gas taxes. The tax we pay is a constant source of disagreement between political parties.

Just as important is how that money is spent. Many countries, including the United States, have social security systems that pay people benefits when they reach retirement age. Some people argue that these payments are wasteful and that better-off people should not receive them. Others argue that "means testing," the best way to find out how wealthy someone is, invades people's privacy. What do you think?

Inflation

Governments sometimes use money as a tool in a different way from simply collecting taxes and making payments. Central banks watch interest rates with an eye toward foreign trade (see pages 30–31) or even buy back bonds to "kickstart" the economy, and governments also have monetary policies with clear goals. These policies are designed to create a stable climate for businesses, so that companies can thrive and produce wealth within a country, and so families can manage their expenses without unexpected shocks.

One of the problems that monetary policy addresses is inflation, or the dramatic rise in prices over time. If prices in a country rise by, say, about 10 percent a year (this was the United States' inflation rate in 1981), then the national currency will lose value over the same period. If wages keep pace with price rises, some people argue that this should not be a problem. But uncertainty about future prices may keep people from investing their money in that country. They may invest in other countries with steadier economies instead.

Most economists today believe that inflation can be caused by too much money in the economy. Economists often advise countries to reduce the national money supply as a first step in the battle against inflation. Governments can have an influence, but the central banks hold the real power, and they look at what is happening abroad when making decisions.

length of time, when the bond is said to mature. Governments also borrow from banks in their own countries. People buy bonds, and banks lend to governments because they are thought to be good risks. In other words, a government is unlikely to default on (not pay) a debt because it can usually find money to repay it by raising taxes. Some countries, however, have unstable governments that cannot sell bonds or find lenders within their own borders. These countries borrow from international institutions such as the World Bank and the International Monetary Fund (IMF).

The World Bank and IMF, along with regional institutions such as the Asian Development Bank and African Development Bank, focus on helping the poorest and least stable countries. Their goal is to help countries help themselves by using loans to build or rebuild their economies.

But those same institutions are often accused of playing politics by forcing countries that borrow money from them to accept strict conditions (controls) on how they spend the money. Those conditions often involve changing the way people in the country borrowing the money have done business for decades or even centuries. Changing those customs overnight can be disruptive, and many countries have suffered riots and even rebellions as a result.

The Ugandan government has used World Bank funds to investigate the possibility of creating a heritage trail in the southwest. The trail would raise awareness of Uganda's rich history and attract tourists.

The Global View

One famous saying about money,

"money makes the world go round," is the title of a song from the musical *Cabaret*. The words of the song tell us that every currency has the power to make the world change, whether it is the mark (Germany's currency before the euro), the Japanese yen, the American buck (slang for dollar), or British pound.

One verse from the song goes:
"A mark, a yen, a buck, or a pound
A buck or a pound
A buck or a pound
Is all that makes the world go around,
That clinking clanking sound
Can make the world go round."

Cabaret is set in the German capital, Berlin, in 1931. The date is important for two reasons. One is that Adolf Hitler's Nazi party was beginning to become more influential in Germany by then, and there is a feeling of menace running through the musical. The second reason is that in 1931, Germany had experienced a crisis with its national currency, the mark. The reasons for this went back several years.

In 1923, Germany went through a time of political unrest when huge strikes closed down many industries for long periods. The government (rather than companies) had to pay the millions of workers who then had no job, so it began printing more and more money. A sudden increase in money supply triggers inflation (see page 26), and prices across Germany began to skyrocket. Eventually, the mark became almost worthless, so people had to take wheelbarrows full of banknotes to pay for a single loaf of bread or piece of meat.

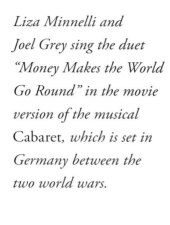

Liza Minnelli and Joel Grey sing the duet "Money Makes the World Go Round" in the movie version of the musical Cabaret, *which is set in Germany between the two world wars.*

The Germans solved this problem within about three years, but the hyperinflation they had suffered remained a painful memory. Hitler convinced many people that he would never allow Germany to be humiliated again.

Central Control

The Germans are not the only people to have heeded the lesson of that brush with hyperinflation. Economists and government leaders around the world

agree that it is vital to keep their national currencies stable. This stability, which means that a dollar or a pound will still have value six months or ten years from now, helps to build confidence in both the currency and the country it represents.

That is where governments and other national structures can play a part. Most countries have central banks that affect the flow and availability of money—especially in banks and other financial institutions. The Federal Reserve (the U.S. central bank), the Bank of England (Britain's central bank), and others use their power to raise and lower interest rates within their countries and to make some transactions easier (or more expensive).

The activity of a country's central bank has effects outside that country. For example, if the Federal Reserve raises interest rates, U.S. banks usually follow its example. As a result, the people who deposit money with these banks receive more interest on their investment. That applies to foreigners as well as U.S. citizens. So if someone sells pounds to buy dollars to invest in a U.S. bank, the dollar becomes worth a bit more (because it is in demand). . . and the pound loses a little of its value against the dollar.

Many other factors affect what are called exchange rates, and foreign exchange dealers (who work for banks or represent customers) play the market by trying to predict whether a particular currency is rising or falling in relation to other currencies.

Weak or Strong

Things become even more complicated when currencies rise or fall sharply. British tourists flocked to the United States in

YOUR MONEY'S WORTH

Euro or No Euro?

One of the fiercest political debates in Britain centers on the euro, and whether Britain should adopt it as a currency. Critics of the euro claim that Britain would suffer, losing jobs and exports while paying higher prices, if the pound were abandoned.

Euro supporters say that the euro would provide Britain with a stronger international currency and also send out a signal that Britain is part of a European team, resulting in Britain being given better terms in the European Union.

KEEP THE £ POUND

NO SURRENDER
STUFF THE EURO
RULE BRITANNIA

2007, knowing that each of their pounds was worth more than $2. Exchange rates had changed dramatically by the end of 2008, when the pound was worth only about $1.48, down from a high of $2.12 about eighteen months earlier. As a result of the change in exchange rates, restaurant meals, hotels, and rental cars in the United States had become more expensive. At the same time, goods that Britain exported to the United States became cheaper because of the fall in value of the pound. This made them more attractive to American buyers and helped British companies.

Governments and central banks need to find a balance between these extremes, but they also know that rises or falls in currency values aren't all bad—or good.

Anti-euro protesters in Britain portray their cause as a patriotic defense of their country's right to manage its own affairs.

The Credit Crunch

Losing a job or being unable to pay

back a loan is a devastating problem for anyone to face. It might take years to return to a stable financial situation. This can happen to countries, too. Germany's hyperinflation, which has recently been repeated in Zimbabwe, had a long-term effect on its outlook. These events may seem relatively insignificant when they affect just one country, but imagine the effect of worldwide economic upheaval.

Personal Account

TAKING RISKS

For decades banks and bank officials had been famous for being careful handlers of other people's money. People felt that money invested in a bank would not only be protected by this careful handling, but that it would grow steadily. In short, banks offered customers a way of becoming a little bit wealthier, but not too fast and without having to take too many chances with their money.

By the 1990s, though, many banks had abandoned their cautious approach as they tried to speed up the process of creating wealth. Lehman Brothers was an example. Under the control of its chief executive Richard (Dick) Fuld, the bank grew richer and richer. Its share price rose from $4 in 1994 to $82 in 2007.

Larry McDonald, a Lehman vice president during that period, explained how Lehman grew so quickly, which is also why it collapsed so spectacularly: "Dick Fuld essentially said to our head risk taker in commercial mortgage-backed securities: 'You've got to take more risk. Risk, risk, risk, risk, risk, and that risk leads to the bottom line (final profit).'"

Opposite: The Great Depression of the 1930s hit northeast England especially hard. Unemployed miners and shipbuilders marched about 310 miles (500 km) from Jarrow to London in October 1936 to protest against poverty.

The world has had several global economic crises. One was the Great Depression of the 1930s, when millions of people around the world lost their jobs, and in many cases, their homes. More recently, countries around the world have been hit by a series of events called the credit crunch, which began in 2007.

Boom and Bust

The credit crunch came at the end of an apparently stable economic time, just like the Great Depression of the 1930s. A period of optimism, when money is lent freely to set up businesses or to buy houses, and when the value of people's investments climbs, is called a boom.

The problem with booms is that people expect them to last forever, so they take risks and lose some of the caution that bankers usually use.

During the early 2000s, house prices rose rapidly in many countries, especially the United States. American banks began lending money to customers who would not usually be offered mortgages because they might have difficulty repaying them. The banks believed that even if these borrowers defaulted (did not repay the loans), the banks could sell the properties to recover the borrowed money.

Then house prices began to fall in late 2006, and when people began to default on their mortgage loans, their houses could not be sold. Banks began to lose lots of money. Then it emerged that other (usually cautious) financial institutions had invested in the banks that were losing money, so they were also losing money. Twenty-first century banking is international, which meant that banks around the world had invested in the American banks and financial institutions that were at the heart of the problems.

Members of the Hong Kong Banking Employees Association stage a protest outside the headquarters of HSBC in February 2009. HSBC was preparing to get rid of 1,000 of its 18,000 Hong Kong staff because of the credit crunch.

Putting More Money In

As well as raising money through taxes, governments can raise cash by issuing bonds. Individuals and—to a much greater extent—banks buy these bonds, which are in effect promises by the government to pay back those buyers with additional interest at a later date. Bonds are considered to be safe investments, which is why they are attractive. But there is a side effect: a lot of banking assets are tied up in these promises, rather than in the form of cash which could be used to make loans to companies and individuals. Many economists believe that the best way to end a recession such as the credit crunch is to get more money moving through the economy. If companies find it easier to take out loans, they can develop and grow more quickly, creating more jobs and helping the country dig its way out of recession. In February 2009, the U.S. Congress used just such a tactic, seeking to jumpstart the economy by passing a $787 billion stimulus bill.

People around the world began to feel the effects when the boom went bust. Banks were at risk and found it hard to pay back their depositors' money. Other banks almost stopped lending altogether, so it became almost impossible for companies to grow, or for new ones to start up. Unemployment grew, and with it grew a widespread resentment toward the bankers many people blamed for the crisis.

During the boom, many high-earning bankers had earned big bonuses by taking risks that led to quick profits. Now, with the crisis in full swing, these same bankers were seen as the culprits. For many observers, the credit crunch really became serious when Lehman Brothers, one of the oldest and most respected U.S. banks, collapsed on September 14, 2008. If that bank went under, who else might follow?

Starting Young

Young people have never been under as much pressure as they are today to learn about money. They need to learn how to make important decisions relatively early in their lives. Even by the age of 12, some students have cell phones and may need to choose the right payment plan.

Later, when college looms, they need to understand about student loans, interest rates, investment programs, and other aspects of the financial world.

Pupils can find advice on all these issues at school, or in local libraries, at a bank, or on the Internet. Most adults welcome questions about how to handle financial affairs. Some young people even find that the places they might visit for advice, such as their local bank, can offer a career that might suit them in later life.

Inside School

Opposite: Young people often start earning by babysitting or doing other locally based jobs. This work helps to prepare them for the important decisions about money they will need to make in later life.

Many government educational advisers would like some form of financial education to be included in the state curricula, the official guidelines setting out what should be taught in schools. The reasons for, and the benefits from, such teaching are obvious. Even very young children are aware that their families have had to cope with the problems of the credit crunch (see pages 32–35). Having a basic grounding in the events that led to the crunch, and the effects it had, could help them make sensible decisions when they are older.

Even without the credit crunch, the financial world has been changing at an unprecedented rate. It is hard for adults to keep track of new methods of payment and a new wave of investment opportunities.

Personal Account **FINANCIAL LITERACY**

Charles R. Schwab is the chairman of the President's Advisory Council on Financial Literacy. In the council's 2008 report, he says,

"We believe the market turmoil and credit crisis of 2008 underscore the critical need for improved financial literacy in the United States. While there are many causes to the economic problems facing the country, it is undeniable that a lack of financial literacy is a contributing factor."

Bill Gates

Bill Gates is one of the best recognized business leaders in the world. Founder of software giant Microsoft, he has consistently been ranked the world's wealthiest person. Gates led the personal computer revolution, which has changed the lives of billions of people.

From an early age, Gates was fascinated by computers. At age 13, he wrote his first computer program. After scoring 1590 out of 1600 on the SAT, he enrolled at Harvard College, but left at age 19 to start his own venture. In the 1980s, this company, Microsoft, developed the first versions of Windows, the world's most widely used operating system.

Until 2006, Gates had primary responsibility for the company's product strategy. He also developed many of its programming products. Gates broadened the company's range, and Microsoft achieved a dominant position in its field. Since then, Gates has been criticized for his aggressive business tactics.

In the past few years, Gates has withdrawn from Microsoft to pursue his charitable interests. As of 2007, he and his wife Melinda had given more than $28 billion to charitable programs. Started in 2000, the Bill and Melinda Gates Foundation has became the world's largest donor. It focuses on global problems, such as AIDS, poverty, scientific research, and technology for schools.

Children today need to learn financial skills far earlier than their parents did. An 18-year-old starting college could earn a degree four years later but may also take out student loans that leave her $20,000 in debt.

Some people are concerned that students are leaving school without the skills to deal with their new responsibilities. Some of the problems are connected to a poor understanding of the basic applications of math. If young people can gain confidence in mathematical skills, they will be better prepared to face the challenges of the wider world.

Translating those skills into practice is a challenge, but educational activists are meeting that challenge in some interesting ways.

Many U.S. children have benefited from programs linking their schools with organizations that promote financial education. One such group, the Jump$tart Coalition for Personal Financial Literacy, started in 1995, helps develop curricula to ensure that basic personal financial management skills are taught in grades K-12. Jump$tart identifies personal finance materials for educational use. Many of the materials are low-cost or free of charge. Teachers use them to support their state's standards in economics, business, math, and family and consumer science.

Gaining confidence with numbers is an essential part of learning how to manage money in later life. Elementary school students can learn to make connections between math lessons and applications in their daily lives.

Into the Future

People often say that no one would have predicted some of the recent developments in communications and transportation 50, or even 30, years ago. The same could be said about the ways in which money and credit are changing. No one predicted the impact of the Internet in 1960 or 1980, or that most people, including teenagers, would have their own cell phones.

The Internet and cell phone technology have played a big part in changing the world of money and credit. Computer users can go online to buy books, airplane tickets, concert tickets, and items on an auction site such as eBay.

This progress is not just centered on people living in the most well-off countries. Many people living in rural Africa and Asia have cell phones that they can use to move money from one bank account to another, sometimes sending amounts to people in other countries.

Expect the Unexpected

The most successful businesses—and business leaders—know that nothing remains the same, and that if they expect the unexpected, they will not be left behind. The same can be said of our understanding of money, and especially, of credit. At the most basic level, people will continue to earn, win, lose, and spend dollars, pounds, and euros. But it is less and less likely that customers 30 or 50 years from now will actually hold coins or paper money in these currencies. All our transactions might well be taking place in the virtual world of the Internet—or whatever has taken its place by then.

Opposite: New technology, such as multi-touch pads, is already revolutionizing the world of money and finance.

YOUR MONEY'S WORTH

It's Your Call

Americans have a saying, "If it ain't broke, don't fix it," which can be applied to buildings, cars, laws, and even economic policies. Nowadays, most people feel that the system that led to the credit crunch probably was broken, or badly in need of repair. Politicians around the world are now calling for changes to the international economic system to prevent a recurrence of the crisis. What measures would you adopt to promote a more sensible view of credit around the world?

Globalization and Microcredit

One of the most important concepts in the twenty-first century is globalization, the way in which the world seems smaller because of advances in technology, communications, and transportation. For people concerned about inequalities in wealth around the world, globalization is a bad thing. They believe that new high-speed and high-tech links make it easier for large companies (from the richest countries) to overwhelm the struggling industries in poorer, developing countries.

But advances do not necessarily lead to a wave of cola and fast food that washes away local businesses in the poorest countries. Instant communication has helped people in the poorest countries improve their lives. One of the most successful advances is microcredit. It establishes banks (or branches of banks) at a local—usually village—level. These banks lend money to local farmers and those starting businesses, i.e. to people who did not have the chance to borrow money before.

Grameen Bank in Bangladesh was the first bank to achieve widespread success with microcredit. The bank's name comes from the local word for village, and that is where much of its business is focused. Its example has been followed by banks around the world. In 2006, the bank and its founder, Muhammad Yunus, were jointly awarded the Nobel Peace Prize.

Despite the rapid rate of change, money in some form will still "make the world go round." And if individuals and businesses need more funds—no matter how those funds are stored or accounted for—they will still need to borrow to make big purchases. So credit will not disappear in the future, either.

In the shorter term, there may be a drop in the risky banking practices that many people believe led to the credit crunch. Big bonuses and investments tied to high-risk mortgages may be less common when the good times return: perhaps the world will have learned a lesson.

Personal Account

BANKER TO THE POOR

The microcredit example set by Muhammad Yunus and the Grameen Bank has been followed by many influential people. Former U.S. president Bill Clinton called on Yunus to help set up microcredit programs to help the poorest people in his own state of Arkansas.

Muhammad Yunus, whose book on microcredit is called Banker to the Poor, believes that the basic justice and fairness of such programs will ensure their success.

"Microcredit is something which is not going to disappear . . . because this is a need of the people. Whatever name you give it, you have to have those financial facilities coming to them because it is totally unfair. . . to deny half the population of the world financial services."

Muhammad Yunus holds his Nobel Peace Prize medal and diploma at Oslo Town Hall after the award ceremony in December 2006.

Glossary

asset   Something of value owned by a person or a business.

barter   An exchange of goods without money.

bill of exchange   A document directing a third party to pay a specific amount of money to a particular person.

boom   A long period of economic confidence, when money is freely available.

budget   A prediction of how much money a family, company, or country will receive and spend in a particular period.

central bank   A country's main monetary authority, which has the power to control interest rates, the supply of money, and other matters related to money and credit.

commodities   Items such as precious metals that have value.

commodity money   A type of money which has value because of the commodity from which it is made, such as gold, silver, or shells.

credit   The granting of a loan, which in turn creates a debt.

credit card   A system of delayed payment, which becomes a loan (to be repaid with interest) if the debt is not paid off by a certain date.

currency   A unit of exchange. The type of money (such as dollar, pound, or euro) used within a country.

default   To fail to pay back (a loan, for example) on time.

developing countries   Less well-off countries, which rely on farming rather than manufacturing for their main income.

economist   A person who specializes in economics, the study of money on a large scale.

exchange rate   How much one currency is worth compared with another.

fiat money   Money that gains its value by being backed by a government.

globalization   The increasing cooperation among countries around the world, or the growing opportunities for companies to spread from one country to another.

government bond   A type of debt a government takes on, selling a document (bond) with the promise to later pay back the purchase price, plus interest.

Great Depression   A period of economic hardship from 1929 to 1939.

inflation   The rise in prices of goods and services in an economy.

interest   A fee paid for borrowing.

International Monetary Fund (IMF)   An international organization that oversees the world financial system and offers loans to the poorest countries.

investments   Something bought in the hope that it will increase in value over time.

mature (in the case of a bond)   To reach its full value.

means testing   Assessing people's income to decide whether they qualify for benefits or other financial help.

monetary   To do with money.

mortgage   A loan to buy a house.

representative money   Money that can be exchanged for the specific amount of gold or silver it represents.

securities   A general term describing financial investments such as bonds and shares.

share   A fraction (or share) of the value of a company, which can be bought and sold.

share price   The price paid for a single share of a company.

transaction   An agreement between a buyer and seller to exchange an asset for an agreed price.

World Bank   An international financial institution that offers loans to developing countries.

Further Reading

Credit Crunch Colin Hynson (Sea-to-Sea Publications, 2010)

Paying without Money Tim Clifford (Rourke Pub., 2009)

Raising Money Barbara Hollander (Heinemann Library, 2008)

Save, Spend, Share: Using Your Money Gerry Bailey and Felicia Law. (Compass Point Books, 2006)

Web Sites

Banking Kids Teens
http://www.bankingkids.com/pages/teen.html

FRB: Federal Reserve Kids Page
http://www.federalreserve.gov/kids/default.htm

Jump$tart Coalition for Personal Financial Literacy
http://www.jumpstartcoalition.org/

Project C.H.A.N.G.E.
http://projectchange.sec.gov/

Index